AIR 200

AIRCRAFT OF THE U.S. BICENTENNIAL

Wayne Mutza

Schiffer Military/Aviation History
Atglen, PA

ACKNOWLEDGMENTS

My special thanks to Hill Goodspeed, National Museum of Naval Aviation (NMNA); Terry Love; Bob Leder, Bell Helicopter Textron, Inc; John Wegg; Bill Sides; David Menard; and the McDonnell-Douglas Corporation. Without their kind and able assistance, this book would not have been possible.

DEDICATION

This book is dedicated to my son Jeffrey, born during the American Bicentennial.

Goals of the American Bicentennial:

"To forge a new national commitment, a new spirit for '76, a spirit which will unite the nation in purpose and dedication to the advancement of human welfare as it moves into its third century."

Book Design by Ian Robertson.

Printed in China.
ISBN: 0-7643-0388-0

We are interested in hearing from authors with book ideas on related topics.

Published by Schiffer Publishing Ltd.
4880 Lower Valley Road
Atglen, PA 19310
Phone: (610) 593-1777
FAX: (610) 593-2002
E-mail: Schifferbk@aol.com
Please write for a free catalog.
This book may be purchased from the publisher.
Please include $3.95 postage.
Try your bookstore first.

AVIATION DURING THE AMERICAN BICENTENNIAL

Let's take a look back in time to the year 1976. For those who were too young to remember, or simply weren't around, here, briefly, is what you missed. That year, one clearly wrought with favorable change, President Gerald Ford implemented a number of changes designed to restructure the U.S. intelligence community. In conjunction with the quest for passage of the Equal Rights Amendment, noteworthy U.S. women were paid overdue homage during a time when others became America's first Anglican priests, Rhodes scholars and Air Force Academy recruits. The year also marked the beginning of Concorde supersonic jet service between the U.S. and Europe. "Jimmy" Carter was elected president of the United States and America's VIKING 1 became the first spacecraft to land on the planet Mars.

The year also hosted literary triumphs such as Alex Haley's ROOTS, Levin's THE BOYS FROM BRAZIL and Woodard and Bernstein's THE FINAL YEARS. Tunes named DREAM WEAVER, STILL CRAZY AFTER ALL THESE YEARS and OB-LA-DI, OB-LA-DA pushed through radio speakers, while THE SHOOTIST, ROCKY and TAXI DRIVER flashed on movie marquees. Video games became the fad that swept the nation.

Though 1976 was a relatively upbeat year, America pondered its position and policies in world affairs, ever mindful of its chaotic exit from Vietnam. She was a nation that had yet to come to terms with its involvement in Vietnam, a nation that, after 30 years of conflict, fell swiftly to communist rule the preceeding year. Normalization talks between the U.S. and Vietnam got underway during late 1976, however, soon after, the U.S. vetoed Vietnam's UN membership application - reconciliation would be a long time in coming.

Most noteworthy about 1976 and perhaps most responsible for the nation's upswing, was the year-long celebration of the Bicentennial of U.S. independence. It was truly an era of good feelings about America which fostered an overdue resurgence of patriotism. The festivities, many of which were grand and glorious, stretched from coast to coast and commemorated countless historic events throughout the year.

Americans, who pride themselves on producing the biggest and the best, made the Fourth of July - Independence Day - a day of remarkable events. In Philadelphia, nearly one million people attended a re-enactment of the signing of the Declaration of Independence, while elsewhere, massive parades filled streets, mammoth fireworks displays thrilled thousands and three major cities hosted oaths of allegiance in mass naturalization ceremonies.

Probably the most spectacular event was the gathering at New York City of more than 200 sailing ships from 34 nations, including 16 of the world's largest windjammers. The splendorous fleet sailed past an honor guard of warships in the harbor and up the Hudson River, as some 30,000 boats jockeyed in the crowded waters for the breathtaking view. Aboard the aircraft carrier U.S.S. FORRESTAL, host ship for the nautical review, were more than 3,000 guests, including foreign dignitaries, members of Congress, the U.S. Cabinet and President Ford.

The patriotic observance was hardly limited to the seafaring community, but extended well into the world of U.S. aviation. Military and civil aircraft alike were transformed into canvasses for every imaginable combination of stars and stripes and red, white and blue. The U.S. military, strong in tradition and patriotic values, bedecked scores of aircraft with a wide variety of schemes and markings. Civil concerns that ranged from private pilots to major airlines also got into the act.

The majority of aircraft that advertised the Bicentennial were flown by the U.S. Air Force and U.S. Navy. Were it a matter of selecting which of the two operated the most aircraft so marked, the Navy would have it, hands down. By sheer proliferation of the series, the McDonnel-Douglas F- 4 PHANTOM stood as the most of any single type to wear Bicentennial dress. The U.S. Army appears to have taken a more conservative stance and the U.S. Coast Guard is not known to have made any concessions to the Bicentennial marking flurry.

The post-Vietnam war era was, for naval aviation, a transitional period during which colorful markings began to reappear. As a refreshing deviation from lackluster warpaint, it was an interval much like that enjoyed by the Navy during the post-Korean war years. And it was to be short-lived, for soon after the Bicentennial, colorful markings would give way, of necessity, to subdued, low-visibility tactical schemes. Those paint jobs (comprising low infra-red compounds), while not visually appealing, did enhance survivability and continue to do so.

The standard basic scheme for naval aircraft during the Bicentennial called for Light Gull Gray over Insignia White, while others, such as those applied to special mission aircraft, used the reverse. The U.S. Air Force deviated somewhat from their familiar "tri-tone" camouflage scheme, a carryover from the war in Southeast Asia. Like the Navy, the Air Force, along with the Army and Marine Corps, would revert to non-specular paint schemes around the end of the decade.

Bicentennial markings typically consisted of the familiar stars and stripes and the national colors red, white and blue. U.S. flags were in abundance along with a grouping of 13 stars, which represented the original 13 colonies. Some aircraft displayed historic flags under which America fought during the Revolutionary War. Other symbols of America included liberty bells and eagles. The official Bicentennial Symbol was chosen from submissions by the nation's leading design firms following a design competition. The symbol formed a white five-pointed star, surrounded by continuous red, white and blue stripes which formed a second star. Circling the double star was the legend, "American Revolution Bicentennial 1776-1976." The double star was symbolic of the two centuries that had passed since the American Revolution. The colorful stripes evoked a feeling of festivity and were suggestive of the furled bunting traditionally used for patriotic celebrations.

Often seen on aircraft during 1976 was the "Minuteman" figure, which represented Revolutionary War militiamen who pledged to fight on a moment's notice. The figure was adopted by the Air National Guard, which carried on the tradition of the Minutemen. Many aircraft, with serial or Bureau numbers that incorporated the numbers "76", were earmarked for use as Bicentennial billboards.

As high-profile ambassadors, the U.S. Air Force aerial demonstration team, the THUNDERBIRDS, was an obvious choice for selection as an official U.S. Bicentennial organization. True to that role, the team's flashy red, white and blue jets had their aircraft numbers on the tail replaced by the Bicentennial symbol. The team's intent to maximize their presentations during the nation's 200th birthday resulted in the reinstatement of a second solo after seven years absence. During 1976, the Thunderbirds flew a total of 102 air shows, surpassing the 2,000 mark.

Even aircraft manufacturers got caught up in the Bicentennial. The McDonnell-Douglas Corporation applied a Bicentennial scheme to one of their F-15 EAGLES, which was one of the stars of the Bicentennial celebration at St. Louis, which drew 800,000 spectators to the city's riverfront on July 4th. The company decided on the colorful F-15 as they felt it was appropriate that an Eagle should carry the national colors that year.

The application of Bicentennial markings to military aircraft, in most cases, was governed either by unit policies and command directives or based solely on personal tastes. Markings ranged from the very simple - a Bicentennial Symbol decal, to the extreme - entire aircraft repainted in dazzling schemes. Those colorful patterns elicited a broad range of reactions; some considered them downright gaudy, while others viewed them as marvelous works of art. One naval historian commented, "The Bicentennial paint jobs have got to be the worst things I've seen this side of a college modern art exhibit."

Regardless of sentiment, the wide variety of markings, plus the relatively short time frame during which they were worn, merit historical documentation. Aircraft decorated for the Bicentennial participated in a historic era and, as such, deserve the attention afforded other segments of U.S. aviation history.

Here, then, is a nostalgic look at the unique aircraft of the U.S. Bicentennial. Though two decades have passed, we would do well by remembering, and even emulating, the astute level of patriotism shown by their aircrew and technicians.

The McDonnell Douglas Corporation capitalized on the Bicentennial celebration to showcase its F-15, which had gone into large-scale production the previous year. (McDonnell Douglas)

Resplendent in its patriotic scheme, the F-15B starred in the Bicentennial celebration at Saint Louis. (McDonnell Douglas)

The "Eagle" performs over the city of Saint Louis on July 4th, 1976. (McDonnell Douglas)

Bell Helicopter turned out this striking UH-IN "Twin Huey" for the Navy during the mid 1970s. (Bell Helicopter)

The opposite pilot's door of the Huey carried the lettering, "P.C. Jarman." (Bell Helicopter)

The Naval Weapons Center at China Lake, California operated this Northrop T-38A in a dazzling scheme during 1976. The T-38A-10 "Talon" was acquired from the U.S. Air Force, where it carried serial number 59-1596. (U.S. Navy)

Detail of the emblem below the Talon's cockpit. (via Terry Love)

The large surfaces of Grumman's C-IA "Trader" provided ample space for Bicentennial decoration. Produced during the 1950s, C-IAs provided carrier transport service into the 1980s. (U.S. Navy)

Probably the most widely publicized "Phantom" in Bicentennial livery was this F-4J Phantom II (BuNo 153088) of Air Test and Evaluation Squadron Four (VX-4) at NAS North Island, California. Even the center-line fuel tank on the belly of "Vandy 76" was consistent with the overall scheme. (McDonnell Douglas)

The eagle caricature was complete with claws, applied to the main landing gear doors. (Mike Grove via NMNA)

Flying over its home base during October 1976, the F-4J shows off its underwing pattern, which paralleled that of the upper surfaces. (NMNA)

The dazzling performer reflects the handiwork of personnel assigned to NAS North Island's Naval Air Rework Facility. (McDonnell Douglas)

Details of "Vandy 76" while visiting the Navy's missile center at Point Mugu, California during February 1976. (U.S. Navy)

The Aero Union Corporation was (and remains) one of the largest operators of vintage radial-engine aircraft, primarily for forest fire-fighting. Among their remarkable inventory was this brilliantly painted DC-4. The Douglas classic is seen here at Chico Municipal Airport in January 1976. (John Brennan)

The same aircraft four months later, complete with Aero Union markings, a name on the nose and retardant tank painted to match the overall scheme. (John Wegg)

View of the fuselage markings on Aero Union's DC-4. (John Brennan)

A TF-104G (S/N 63-13076) of the 69th Tactical Fighter Training Squadron, 58th Tactical Fighter Training Wing during March 1976. The unit served as a West German Air Force training squadron at Luke AFB, Arizona. (Rotramel via Dave Menard)

View of the "Starfighter's" wing tip fuel tank fin (foreground) and elaborate tail art. (Rotramel via Dave Menard)

The artist's inscription appears on the lower left portion of the F-104's tail fin. (Centurion via Dave Menard)

This 1958 vintage T-33A of the 57th Fighter Interceptor Squadron (FIS) wears the shield of its parent command, the Air Defense Command (ADC), and a Bicentennial symbol on the center fuselage. (MAP)

VA-122 (Attack Squadron 122) at NAS Lemoore was one of only two Fleet Replacement Squadrons that operated A-7Es after the Navy standardized its light attack squadrons. The "Flying Eagles" began converting to TA-7Cs in 1978. The red, white and blue fuselage lettering, seen here on the squadron commander's aircraft, was a common Navy practice during the Bicentennial. (MAP)

A Lockheed S-3A "Viking" of VS-41 over San Clemente, California during July 1976. The "VS" designation identified Sea Control Squadrons equipped with carrier-based anti-submarine warfare (ASW) aircraft. (U.S. Navy via NMNA)

The port side of the same aircraft, with its wings folded. (Candid Aero Files)

The Viking's yellow rattlesnake and legend, "Don't Tread On Me", is taken from the Gadsden flag, which was the personal ensign of the U.S. Navy's first commodore, Esek Hopkins. The shamrock tails in the background depict VS-41's standard markings. VS-41 was based at NAS North Island. (U.S. Navy via NMNA)

The wing tip fuel tanks of this F-104G of the 69th TFTS, 58th TFTW were painted for the Bicentennial. (MAP)

The patriotic scheme of the U.S. Air Force Flight Demonstration Team, "Thunderbirds", was slightly altered to incorporate the Bicentennial emblem on the tail fin of the T-38As. (MAP)

The Thunderbirds team logo was placed on the starboard side of the aircraft. (MAP)

During the Bicentennial, the Thunderbirds flew 1968-model T-38As, making them T-38A-75s. A total of ten were assigned to the team, having serial numbers 68-8100, 8106, 8131, 8156, 8174, 8175, 8176, 8177, 8182 and 8184. Four of those were lost during a formation crash, which claimed the lives of all four pilots, on 18 January 1982. (MAP)

Known to be one of the very few Republic F-105s that displayed Bicentennial markings, this example of the New Jersey Air National Guard (ANG) wore a colorful tail with its otherwise drab scheme. The F-105B belonged to the 141st Tactical Fighter Squadron, 108th Tactical Fighter Wing. (Hugh R. Muir via Terry Love)

Evergreen operated this Lockheed L-188 "Electra" during the Bicentennial. The stars were applied over black and green stripes. (Candid Aero Files)

A pair of California-based T-2C "Buckeye" trainers of VT-26 differed only in the color of the "76" on their tails. (Candid Aero Files)

Naval Strike students received their intermediate training in the T-2C Buckeye, which was phased out in favor of the T-45. (MAP)

A North American OV-1OA "Bronco" (BuNo 155498) of VMO-1 carries a decorated center-line fuel tank. (MAP)

This F-4N of VF-151 exemplified the Navy practice of modifying squadron markings with those of a patriotic scheme. The Phantom was the squadron commander's aircraft. (Candid Aero Files)

The Bicentennial tail markings of this F-4J of VMFA-232 "Red Devils" are balanced by the round emblem on the nose. (Hugh Muir via Terry Love)

This F-4J was flown by the "Crusaders" of VMFA-122. (Hugh Muir via Terry Love)

This RF-4B belonged to Marine Fighter Photographic Squadron Three (VMFP-3), based at MCAS El Toro. The attractive Phantom II carried the Marine Corps emblem on the tail fin. (Tom Doll)

In contrast, this RF-4B from the same unit wears a red fuselage banner and U.S. flags on the tail. Thirteen red stars were applied to each white-painted tail stabilator. (Harry Gann via NMNA)

VF-161's red and black squadron markings were replaced on this F-4N (BuNo 151433) by red, white and blue. Unusual is the "1976" positioned to the left of the tail code. (Hugh Muir via Terry Love)

The Carrier Air Wing commander's aircraft, identified by the "100" on the nose, which appears in red, white and blue. Thirteen gold stars on a blue band frame the tail code, the first letter of which signifies a Pacific Fleet assignment. (Hugh Muir via Terry Love)

Markings on this F-4J of VMFA-312 were representative of the unit name "Checkerboards." The unit designator, which clashed with the bold unit colors, was applied in red, white and blue on the upper fuselage. (Hugh Muir via Terry Love)

During 1974, the "Warlords" of VMFA-451 flew F-4Js which made liberal use of blue trim and white stars. The Bicentennial dates on the center fuselage contrast well with the aircraft's overall gray. (J.E. Michaels via Terry Love)

The squadron commander's aircraft of the same unit with a center-line fuel tank, also trimmed in blue. Although VMFA-451 was based at MCAS Beaufort, its Phantoms wore the tail code of its Atlantic Fleet carrier air wing and displayed the carrier's name from which it operated. (Hugh muir via Terry Love)

In addition to the Bicentennial "pretzel", other tail markings identify this F-4J as a commander's aircraft. The Phantom is seen here at NAS Miramar on 3 July 1976. (Bruce Trombecky via NMNA)

An F-4J of the "Grim Reapers" at NAS Miramar on 3 July 1976. Barely visible on the red, white and blue tail are the dates "1776-1976." (Bruce Trombecky via NMNA)

This F-4B was assigned to VMFA-351, which also served as the Marine Air Reserve Training Detachment (MARTD) at NAS Atlanta. (Hugh Muir via Terry Love)

Aircraft number Four from the same unit was a F-4B in identical markings. (Candid Aero Files)

This F-4B of VF-51's "Screaming Eagles" illustrates the longevity of some Bicentennial markings. Bureau Number 150476 is seen here during December 1980, its bold markings none the worse for wear. (Hugh Muir via Terry Love)

Positioned at center fuselage of this F-4J of VF-103 is a variation of the original "Betsy Ross Flag", which became the first national ensign. (Hugh Muir via Terry Love)

Very often, the commander's mount was a unit's only lavishly decorated aircraft. Such may have been the case with this F-4J of the VMFA-115 "Silver Eagles." A silver eagle soars on the fuselage between the unit designation and Bureau Number. (Hugh Muir via Terry Love)

This view of the same aircraft shows the fine detail of stripes and stars on the wing and stabilator tips. (Jerry Geer)

This F-4N of VF-III "Sundowners" is an example of the Navy practice of modifying squadron markings for the Bicentennial. (U.S. Navy via NMNA)

The abundance of markings applied to this F-4J detracts from its Tactical Paint Scheme (TPS). The hash mark under the Battle Efficiency "E" on the splitter vane signifies a succeeding award. Aircraft assigned to carrier air wings usually wear the name of the ship to which they are assigned. (Robert L. Lawson via NMNA)

Among the markings on this F-4B of VF-301 is the Bicentennial symbol surrounded by red, white and blue lettering which reads, "United States of America 1776 1976." The aircraft side number ends in double zero (called "double nuts" in Navy parlance), indicating an air wing or group commander's aircraft. The row of color stars at the base of the tail fin represent the ID colors of squadrons that comprise the group. The stylized tail code is "ND", denoting assignment to the Pacific Fleet. (Hugh Muir via Terry Love)

Though not as frequently photographed as their military contemporaries, aircraft painted for the Bicentennial flourished in civil aviation. Seen at Oakland, California, in November 1976, this Piper PA-23 Apache-Geronimo conversion was operated by Sierra Aero. (John Wegg)

A Beech T-34B "Mentor" of the NAS North Island Flying Club. (NMNA)

Helicopter Anti-submarine Sqaudron Eight (HS-8), known as the "Eightballers", operated this Sikorsky SH-3D with a patriotic theme. Bureau Number 154111 is seen here over San Diego, near its home base NAS North Island. The numbers "76" appeared on the nose and a thin red stripe followed the hull's chine line. (NMNA)

Three Overseas National Airlines DC-8s are known to have flown with special Bicentennial markings. Besides this DC-8-21 was identically marked N1776GR. A DC-8-32, named "Independence", displayed a red and white-striped aft fuselage, along with a circle of 13 blue stars on the tail fin. (Terry Love)

ONA patterned the aft portion of this DC-8-21 after the flag of the confederacy, a group of 11 southern states that seceded from the U.S. in 1860-61. (Terry Love)

The Navy used Lockheed S-3 "Vikings" to equip ASW squadrons. This S-3A of VS-29, based at NAS North Island, had a Bicentennial ensign incorporated into a viking ship, the squadron emblem. (Robert L. Lawson via NMNA)

Besides the liberty bell adorning the main landing gear door of this S-3A, Safety, ASW and Battle Efficiency awards are carried behind the cockpit. The VS-21 Viking is accompanied by the aircraft it replaced, a specially modified Grumman S-2G "Traoker" of VS-37. (U.S. Navy via NMNA)

Like many USAF multi-engine aircraft, this NKC-135A is modestly decked out for the Bicentennial. The Boeing jet was assigned to the 4952nd Test Squadron, 4950th Test Wing of the Aeronautical Systems Division as an electronic agressor aircraft. (MAP)

Though this RF-4C wears no Bicentennial trim, its travel pod on the inboard pylon is fully decorated. The Phantom was assigned to the 1st TRS, 10th TRW at Alconbury, England. (MAP)

Besides a Bicentennial symbol, this F-4C of the 57th FIS wears red, white and blue stripes on the tail fin tip. (MAP)

Sporting a Bicentennial emblem, this 4th TFW F-4E is armed with four AIM-9B Sidewinder missiles. (MAP)

The stripes on the white tail fin were repeated on the stabilators of this F-4C (S/N 63-7576) of the 57th FIS. (MAP)

An F-4D (S/N 66-7617) of the 49th TFW at Holloman AFB, NM. (MAP)

Units abroad proudly displayed patriotic colors. U.S. Air Force Europe (USAFE) included the 22nd TFS, 36th TFW, based at Bitburg, Germany, whose F-4Es wore colorful tail markings. Note the mechanic's tool box similarly marked. (Candid Aero Files)

This view of the same aircraft shows a change in markings. The Bicentennial emblem is missing from the splitter vane and the Mig stars have been enlarged. In addition, the outer wing panels were painted red, white and blue along with crew names on the canopy rail. (Candid Aero Files)

This F-4C (S/N 63-7676) belonged to the commander of the 4th TFTS, 58th TFTW at Luke AFB, Arizona. Since Phantoms accounted for the majority of Mig kills during the Southeast Asian war, it's not surprising that two kill markings appear on the splitter vane below the cockpit. (MAP)

F-4C of the 57th FIS. The complete serial number was 63-7685. (MAP)

Naval painters took advantage of the "Stoof's" massive surfaces and applied a Bicentennial color scheme which incorporated more than 100 stars. The US-2B was assigned to Training Squadron 31. (Bob Esposito)

The Grumman E-2 "Hawkeye" was an early warning/communications aircraft. While assigned to the USS MIDWAY, this E-2B wore an interesting patriotic pattern on the forward fuselage. (U.S. Navy)

Identified as a commander's aircraft by the "double nuts" below the cockpit, this Douglas C-117D operated from MCAS Beaufort, South Carolina in this appealing scheme. (Bruce Stewart via Nick Williams)

The colorful paint job on this A-7D of the New Mexico Air National Guard was short-lived following a "difference of opinion" between command staff and the personnel who decided to paint it. (Centurion via Dave Menard)

Wearing a design that was stylish for an old bird, this T-33A had the serial number 57-761. After 13 years as a primary USAF trainer, the T-33 went on to serve the Air National Guard and Reserves. (Slowiak via Dave Menard)

This view of the "Shooting Star" shows the position of the wrap-around stripes on the landing gear doors and a star on the wing tip tank. (Slowiak via Dave Menard)

The North American T-28 "Trojan" served as a primary Navy trainer during the Bicentennial era. A number of them served in patriotic livery, such as this flashy T-28B of Training Squadron Two (VT-2), based at Whiting Field, Florida. (U.S. Navy via NMNA)

Few U.S. Army aircraft are known to have sported Bicentennial decor, making this Huey quite the exception to the Army's conservative approach to lavish markings. The Bell UH-IB was photographed at Hunter AAF, Georgia. (Tom Patterson via Terry Love)

The clever design, which incorporated the numbers "76", also included a 25th Infantry Division emblem on the tail. (Tom Patterson via Terry Love)

Piedmont Airlines used this motif during the Bicentennial, seen here on one of their Boeing 737-200s. (Ronald Macklin)

Training Squadron Ten (VT-10) flew this beautiful T-39D "Sabreliner" from its home base of NAS Pensacola. The sleek nose design uses the usual number of 13 stars. (MAP)

Details of the Sabreliner's tail art. (L.B. Sides)

This F-8A is evidence that "gate guards" were not exempt from Bicentennial schemes. The Crusader also served as a sign post for MAG-49's commander. (MAP)

The TA-4J was the two-seat variant of the Douglas Skyhawk. The banner of the emblem below the cockpit reads "FITRON 43", the Navy acronym for Fighter Sqaudron 43. (MAP)

Training Squadron Seven painted this TA-4J in a classy scheme. Based at NAS Meridian, VT-7 was the last training squadron to operate Skyhawks. (Candid Aero Files)

A number of Texas Air National Guard aircraft proudly displayed the markings seen on the center fuselage of this F-IOIB "Voodoo" of the 111th FIS. The red, white and blue banner was added during exercise WILLIAM TELL 76. (MAP)

As proof that Bicentennial markings were not limited to high performance aircraft, the tail of this 63rd MAW C-141A (S/N 66-176) is trimmed in blue with 13 stars. (MAP)

Though simply marked, this T-37B of the 38th TFW displays its serial number, 58-1976. "City of Columbus" is painted on the nose. (Hugh Muir via Terry Love)

The "Spirit of 76" sometimes went beyond aircraft markings as seen by the exhaust cover of this 49th FIS F-106A. (L.B. Sides)

An F-106A (S/N 59-053) of the Air Defense Command (ADC). (L.B. Sides)

Introduced during the early 1970s, Grumman's F-14 "Tomcat" was hailed as the Navy's premier fighter. It was also considered the most glamorous, a fact difficult to dispute in view of this F-14A of VF-124, trimmed for the Bicentennial. (Candid Aero Files)

An RF-8G of Photo Reconnaissance Squadron 63. The Crusader's Pacific Fleet tail code is framed by flowing bands of red, white and blue. (Candid Aero Files)

The serial number of this high visibility Cessna T-37B is 59-0376. (Robert Pickett)

Seen here at Forbes ANGB, this C-131 of the Iowa National Guard uses attractive demarcation stripes. (via Nick Williams)

A WC-130E of the 54th Weather Reconnaissance Sqaudron. The Bicentennial emblem is displayed in the standard location for Hercules aircraft. (Candid Aero Files)

A North American F-100F of the Arkansas Air National Guard. Barely visible above the razorback painted on the Super Sabre's nose is a "76" incorporating 13 white stars. (Benjamin Knowles, Jr.)

This 1956 vintage F-100D was later converted to a QF-100. Besides liberal amounts of orange trim, this weathered Super Sabre wears the special ANG emblem below the cockpit. (L.B. Sides)

A C-141B uses a liberty bell as the background for the last two digits of its serial number, 63-8076. The "Starlifter" belonged to the 438th Military Airlift Wing (MAW) of the Military Airlift Command (MAC). (Candid Aero Files)

Having serial number 57-1776, this F-102A was an obvious candidate for Bicentennial trim, which was applied over its Vietnam war era camouflage. The "Deuce" served as a gate guard at NAS Keflavik, Iceland. (MAP)

Besides a red, white and blue rudder, this T-37B of the 46th Air Defense Wing (ADW) carried a large Bicentennial symbol just behind the cockpit. (MAP)

A T-38A Talon (S/N 69-7076) of the Air Training Command (ATC). (Centurion via Dave Menard)

This T-38A wore a radical design for the Bicentennial. (MAP)

This star-studded Smith 600 Aerostar paid tribute to the Bicentennial, right down to its registration. The "bizjet" is seen at Dallas-Addison during November 1979. (Dan Hagedorn)

Complete with a four-star placard (in the cockpit) and carpeted entry steps, this T-39B served as the transport for the commander of the ADC. Sharing the tail fin with the Bicentennial symbol is the ADC emblem. (MAP)

Besides the attractive tail, the nose landing gear door of this F-IIIE carried a Bicentennial symbol and the greeting, "Happy Birthday America." The "Raven', like the majority of those built, was assigned to the 20th TFW at Upper Heyford, England. (MAP)

The unique finish was appropriate for this RF-84K since only 25 of the type were produced. This example was preserved at Baker AFB, Arkansas, where it is seen during 1977. (MAP)

A standard ANG emblem on the tail was complemented by its commemorative version below the cockpit on this F-1OOD of the Indiana ANG. (Candid Aero Files)

Unit markings and informational data left little room for the Bicentennial symbol on this F-106A of the 87th FIS. (via Terry Love)

Among the many markings on the tail of this EB-57B is a "76" formed by stars on a blue field. This 1952 vintage Martin was flown by the 134th DSES of the Vermont ANG. (MAP)

This EB-57E's unit designation, the 17th DSES, is incorporated into patriotic markings on the underwing pods. (MAP)

An EB-57E from the same unit, at Malstrom AFB, Montana, displays wrap-around fuselage stripes with a Bicentennial symbol. (MAP)

This well-maintained UH-IN of the 67th ARRS wore Bicentennial symbols on the pilots' doors. The cabin doors featured the squadron insignia and an outstanding unit citation. (MAP)

A simple design on the rudder enhanced the inherent beauty of this A-7B, seen at Buckley ANG Base, Colorado. (A. Swanberg)

A narrow banner finished off the trim of this Corsair II of Attack Squadron ("ATKRON") 46. (L.B. Sides)

An old naval ensign decorated the rudders of VA-46's A-7s. (L.B. Sides)

Leading this trio of TA-4Js past Mount Rushmore is the commander of Training Wing Three. (J.W. Alber)

The commander's Skyhawk is clearly identified by the "double zero" side number, fuselage banner and multi-colored rudder. The large "C" on the tail signified CTW-3 at NAS Chase Field, which was disestablished during 1992. (J.W. Alber)

Not one part of this TA-4J was overlooked when it was decorated in the national colors. (L.B. Sides)

Bicentennial markings on this General Dynamics F-IIIF were plentiful. Various patterns of stars and stripes are visible on the tail, engine intake and aft fuselage. The F-IIIF was similar to the F-IIID, but combined the best electronic features of the F-IIIE and F-IIIA. This example, serial number 70-2376, belonged to the 389th TFS of the 366th TFW at Mountain Home AFB, Idaho. (MAP)

A McDonnell F-IOIB "Voodoo" of the Oregon ANG wears both ANG emblems. (L.B. Sides)

Big on pride and tradition, the Texas Air National Guard was known for its colorfully marked aircraft. This Voodoo was no exception as it flys the Texas flag, along with the bicentennial ANG emblem during 1976. (L.B. Sides)

More often associated with ANG aircraft, a Minuteman and banner with 13 stars graces the massive tail of a Lockheed P-3A "Orion" of VP-92. (L.B. Sides)

The 13 stars on the tail fin of this T-2C of VT-23 encircle a Minuteman figure. (Candid Aero Files)

Bicentennial markings are among the many applied to this VT-23 "Buckeye." (via L.B. Sides)

The classic lines of this T-33A were highlighted by fore and aft ANG emblems. The red, white and blue "NGB" high on the tail fin signify assignment to the National Guard Bureau at Washington, D.C. (Jim Sullivan)

The gleaming finish of this T-33A of the National Guard Bureau is complemented by both ANG emblems. A one-star placard in the cockpit indicates its use as a general's hack. (Fred Harl)

A 1953 vintage T-33A of the NGB at Andrews AFB. (Bill Curry)

A T-33A dressed in high visibility and Bicentennial markings at Westover AFB. (L.B. Sides)

Ever the vision of jet age beauty, a polished metal T-33A of the 48th FIS rests on the ramp at Tyndall AFB. (L.B. Sides)

Details of the same aircraft's tail markings. (L.B. Sides)

During the Bicentennial period, the Air Force seldom ventured beyond the application of a Bicentennial emblem, possibly for fear of spoiling an aircraft's inherent good looks. In the case of this beautiful T-33 of the 24th Air Division, that thinking would certainly have been justified. (L.B. Sides)

In addition to their support role, T-33As were used by the 111th FIS of the Texas ANG from 1957 to 1976 for the ANG Jet Instrument Training School. (L.B. Sides)

Carrier Airborne Early Warning Squadron (VAW) 88's E-2B "Hawkeye" over Lake Havasua, Arizona during 1976. The Hawkeye's brightly painted "rotodome" left no doubt about VAW-88's soaring level of patriotism. (NMNA)

Close examination of these F-4s and A-7s reveal seven tails displaying Bicentennial markings. The Phantoms and Corsair IIs were parked on the flight deck of the USS FRANKLIN D. ROOSEVELT (CVA-42) during February 1977. (Pete Clayton)

The squadron commander's TA-4J of VF-126 on final approach to NAS Miramar during March 1977. (Robert L. Lawson via NMNA)

A Bicentennial symbol does little to disrupt the sleek lines of this T-39A of the 89th MAW. (MAP)

A S-3A of VS-21 at NAS North Island during March 1976. The Viking's main landing gear doors are adorned with a liberty bell and red, white and blue stripes. (Bruce Trombecky via NMNA)

North American's F-86 "Sabre", of Korean war fame, served the Air National Guard until 1965. This F-86D (S/N 52-10115), which served as gate guard at Chandler AFB, Arizona during the 1970s, wore a Bicentennial emblem in addition to red, white and blue stripes. (MAP)

A Northrop F-5E of the 58th TFTW. (MAP)

A Bicentennial symbol was added to the profusion of red trim applied to this T-39A of the Air Force Communications Service. (Candid Aero Files)

This F-100D wears the standard ANG emblem on the tail and the Bicentennial version on the fuselage. The "Super Sabre", which hailed from the 112th TFS, 180th TFG of the Ohio National Guard, is seen here at Toledo's Express Airport during July 1977. (MAP)

Eastern Airlines operated this Boeing 727 which is seen at Miami during July 1976. The Bicentennial artwork incorporated nine historic flags which circle the legend, "1776-What So Proudly We Hail-1976." (MAP)

An HC-130N of the 67th ARRS, 39th ARRW during 1976. (MAP)

An A-4L of Marine Fighter Attack Squadron 142. VMFA-142 "Flying Gators" traded in their Skyhawks for F/A-18A Hornets. (Candid Aero Files)

A RA-5C of Reconnaissance Attack Squadron (RVAH) 12. Besides markings on the Vigilante's slab-sided intake, crew names appeared within red, white and blue stripes behind the cockpit. Though equipped with an external electronic package, the recon "Vig" maintained an attack capability. (Candid Aero Files)

This T-39D served as the Air Wing commander's aircraft while assigned to Attack Squadron 122. Pictured during August 1976, the Sabreliner wears an interesting pattern on its nose and tail. (via Nick Williams)

This "Thud's" short nose radome identifies it as a F-105B day fighter. (Bob Esposito)

Bright trim contrasted sharply with this OH-6A's overall olive drab finish in 1976. Lettering on the "Cayuse's" pilots' doors read, "Rhode Island Army National Guard." (Candid Aero Files)

This A-4B displayed at NAS Lemoore during the 1970s was fully decorated for the Bicentennial, right down to the Bullpup AGM missiles. (MAP)

Home port for this EA-6B of VAQ-132 "Scorpions" was NAS Whidbey Island, Washington, which is highlighted on the colorful graphic below the cockpit. Electronic jamming pods are carried under the "Prowler's" wings. (Hugh Muir via Terry Love)

Nearly 100 Intruders were modified by Grumman or the Navy as tankers, which were designated KA-6Ds. While deployed aboard the USS INDEPENDENCE, this example wore a detailed Bicentennial emblem on the rudder. (MAP)

A lineup of VA-196 A-6Es wearing stylized "76s" on their rudders, at NAS Barbers Point, Hawaii during August 1976. (Roy Lock via NMNA)

Red and blue pin stripes, plus a liberty bell, trimmed out this EA-6B of VAQ-136 "Gauntlets." (Hugh Muir via Terry Love)

Simple but attractive Bicentennial markings accented this Prowler of VAQ-137 deployed aboard USS AMERICA during 1980. (Hugh Muir via Terry Love)

Marine All Weather Attack Squadron 121 "Green Knights" operated A-6E long-range all-weather attack Intruders from NAS Miramar. (Hugh Muir via Terry Love)

An A-6E of VA-128 sports dual flags and dates on its rudder. (Hugh Muir via Terry Love)

An A-6E of VA-196 during 1978. (Hugh Muir via Terry Love)

The dates 1776-1976 appear below the liberty bell on the nose of this EA-6B. (Hugh Muir via Terry Love)

A unique Bicentennial shield was applied to the forward fuselage of this A-6A. (NMNA)

The white trim on this engine gray CH-46D includes Bicentennial markings on the forward rotor pylon. The "Sea Knight" belonged to Helicopter Combat Support Squadron Three (HC-3) "Pack Rats.' (Art LeGare via NMNA)

North American T-28Bs assigned to the Station Flight at NAF Washington used these standard tail markings during the Bicentennial. (Candid Aero Files)

Having been relegated to desert storage in Arizona during 1976, this T-28B had a storage code applied to the canopy frame. (MAP)

Seen at NAS North Island on 26 September 1976, this S-3A of VS-22 wore a yellow "Don't Tread On Me" ensign on its lower tail. (Bruce Trombecky via NMNA)

Grumman's "Greyhound" was aptly named. Known simply as the "COD", for Carrier Onboard Delivery, the type was developed solely for carrier logistics. This C-2A of VR-24 displayed Bicentennial markings near the cockpit. (Bruce Trombecky via NMNA)

Few Lockheed Orions are known to have sported Bicentennial markings, however, this P-3A wore a large "Don't Tread On Me" ensign on the forward fuselage. Patrol Squadron 44, "The Pelicans", was stationed at NAS Brunswick. (Jim Sullivan via NMNA)

True to their name, the "Liberty Bells", Orions of VP-66 wore a large liberty bell on their tails, surrounded by 13 stars. This P-3A is pictured at NAS Miramar on 13 March 1976. (Bruce Trombecky via NMNA)

A Bell UH-1F of the 37th ARRS, wearing the official Bicentennial emblem on its tail boom, flies over flood-ravaged land in search of stranded persons. (Bell Helicopter Textron)

Resplendent in its patriotic theme, this TA-4J was flown by the commander of VF-126. The Skyhawk was called "Hawk One." (Candid Aero Files)

Completing this TA-4J's beautiful scheme was red, white and blue gothic-style lettering under the cockpit which read, "Cdr Ray Russell Hawk One", indicating the squadron commander's aircraft. (Dave Steinbacher Collection)

Six ANG squadrons were equipped with Convair F-106 "Delta Darts" during the Bicentennial period, however, none could compare with this F-106A, boasted by the 159th FIS, 125th FIG of the Florida ANG. Lettering surrounding the emblem on the underwing pods read, "This Is My Country 1776-1976." (K. Buchanan via Dave Menard)

Underside view of the same aircraft. (via Dave Menard)

Starboard view of serial number 58-0760. (Candid Aero Files)

So detailed was the Dart's special scheme that tiny stars were applied to the needle-like nose probe. (L.B. Sides)

After 28 years, the Corsair II was retired from U.S. naval service in 1994. This A-7E hailed from VA-66 "Waldos." (Bruce Trombecky via NMNA)

VA-125 "Barn Owls" deployed with A-7Bs aboard the USS ROOSEVELT for a "Med" cruise from October 1976 to April 1977. The canopy frame, along with much of the Corsair II's lettering, was trimmed in red, white and blue. (Bruce Trombecky via NMNA)

A flight of RF-8Gs of Photographic Reconnaissance Squadron 63 (VFP-63) with red, white and blue-painted tails. (LCDR Ruby via NMNA)

Wrapped around the mace (which was VA-27's unit emblem) on the tail of this A-7E Corsair II is a red, white and blue pennant with the figures "76." (Roy Lock via NMNA)

The VA-97 "Warhawks" flew these Bicentennial-marked A-7Es aboard the "Big E" during a WESPAC cruise from July 1976 to March 1977. (Roy Lock via NMNA)

This colorfully trimmed example served VA-22 aboard the USS CORAL SEA. The emblem on the tail, which represents the unit name "Fighting Redcocks", is repeated on the forward fuselage. After light attack squadron realignment, the A-7E remained as the only single-seat variant of the Corsair II in service. (MAP)

The legend "1776-1976" was added to the white wrap-around stripe just forward of this A-7B's wing. The VA-72 Corsair II is pictured at NAS North Island during March 1976. (Robert L. Lawson via NMNA)

All tail colors of this RF-8G were red, white and blue. The photo reconnaissance variant of the "Crusader" was flown by Detachment 3 of VFP-63. (Bruce Trombecky via NMNA)

The VA-153 "Blue Tail Flies" operated A-7Bs from the USS ROOSEVELT in the Med from October 1976 to April 1977. Besides a Bicenten-nial emblem on the tail, this A-7 wears a "Battle E" with succeeding award for gunnery. (Bruce Trombecky via NMNA)

After the fall of South Vietnam in 1975, the U.S. Navy restructured its light attack squadrons, which involved transferring the A-7s to Reserve units. This A-7A was operated by the Naval Air Reserve at Point Mugu, California. The "double nuts' on the tail fin tip were red, white and blue. Barely visible on the main landing gear door is a stylish "1776-1976." (Pete Mancus via NMNA)

The wings of this A-7B of VA-125 are edged with red, white and blue stripes. The red and white-edged tail fin is blue with a red and white rudder. (Bruce Trombecky via NMNA)

Assigned to the 318th FIS at Paine Field, Washington, this F-106A, named "The Freedom Bird", guarded America's northern skies in these markings. The inboard half of the wing-mounted fuel tanks were light gray. (Centurion via Dave Menard)

A F-106A of the 49th Fighter Interceptor Squadron (FIS). (Candid Aero Files)

The same aircraft after a change in tail marking colors, sans underwing pods and nose Bicentennial emblem. (Centurion via Dave Menard)

A F-106A (S/N 59-0083) of the 49th FIS. (MAP)

The tail of this F-106A of the 84th FIS is decorated with an interesting red, white and blue design that incorporates the unit's designation, surrounded by the customary 13 stars. (MAP)

Grumman's "Trader" was developed during the 1950s to fill a need for a larger carrier transport. Before Navy Tactical Paint Schemes became the norm (after 1980), Traders seemed to epitomize the Navy's reputation for colorfully marked aircraft. Decked out for the Bicentennial, this C-IA was assigned to NAS Lemoore, California. (Candid Aero Files)

Its engine nacelles meticulously painted to represent the U.S. flag, this attractive C-IA is embellished with numerous markings denoting assignment to "Blue Ghost", the USS LEXINGTON. (Robert L. Lawson via NMNA)

Wearing a patriotic "triple zero" on the nose, this C-1A was assigned to NAS Lemoore during the late 1970s. (MAP)

Markings other than those with a Bicentennial theme on this C-1A leave no doubt that the Trader operated from the USS LEXINGTON, better known as the "Blue Ghost." (via Dave Steinbacher)

The same aircraft, its wings folded for storage, awaits restoration at the Naval Aviation Museum at NAS Pensacola. (Bill Devins)

The tail of this US-2D deviated greatly from those of others assigned to Washington (seen in the background). These "Tracker" variants were modified by the Navy for target-towing and utility. (Candid Aero files)

Helicopter Antisubmarine Squadron 74 flew this Sikorsky SH-3G adorned with a large patriotic ensign. HS-74 Reserve was disestablished on 1 January 1985 and the SH-3G version of the Sea King has disappeared from the Navy inventory. (MAP)

MISCELLANEOUS

*The official symbol of the American Bicen-
tennial.*

On a similar note, the year 1976 marked the 50th anniversary of commercial aviation, commemorated by this U.S. postage stamp.

A cross section of naval aviation during the Bicentennial graced the cover of the December issue of Naval Aviation News. All the aircraft pictured on the cover are featured in this book. (U.S. Navy)

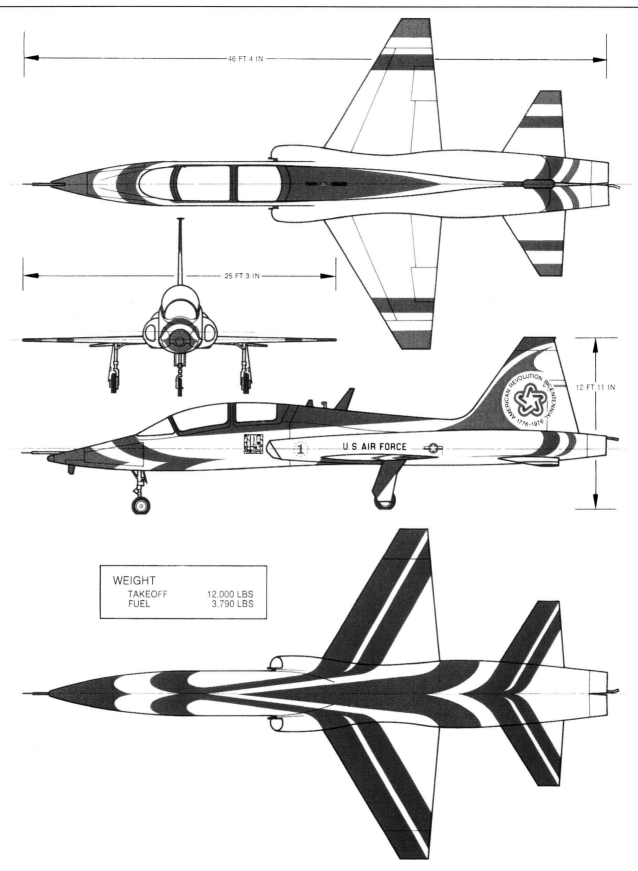

WEIGHT
TAKEOFF   12,000 LBS
FUEL   3,790 LBS

Details of the special color scheme worn by the Northrop T-38A "Talons" flown by the USAF "Thunderbirds."

*Version of the Air National Guard emblem designed specially for the Bicentennial.
The emblem was applied to numerous ANG aircraft.*

Design used by Bell Helicopter during the Bicentennial.

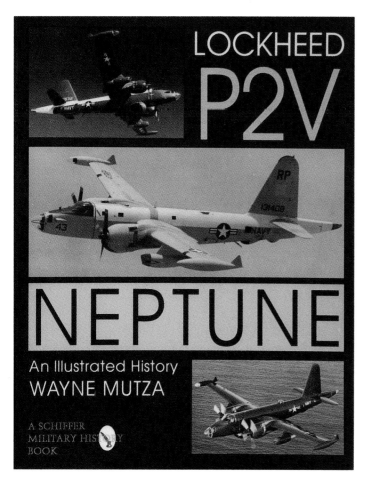

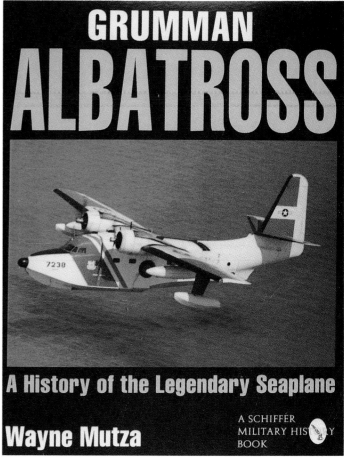

LOCKHEED P2V NEPTUNE:
AN ILLUSTRATED HISTORY

Wayne Mutza

This long overdue account provides an extraordinary amount of insight into the Neptune's lengthy history, beginning with its inception during World War II to the present day survivors. More than 1,000 examples were built, many of which thrive today as fire bombers and warbirds. Presented here for the first time are the many fascinating details describing Neptune service with non-U.S. air arms and obscure operations. Clearly evident is the in-depth research that makes this extensive volume accurate, detailed and readable.
Size: 8 1/2" x 11"
over 400 b/w & color
photographs,
approx. 176 pages, hard cover
ISBN: 0-7643-0151-9 $49.95

GRUMMAN ALBATROSS:
A HISTORY OF THE LEGENDARY
SEAPLANE
Wayne Mutza.

The Albatross was the premier fixed-wing rescue aircraft for the U.S. Air Force and Coast Guard.

Size: 8 1/2" x 11" over 200 b/w and color photographs, line schemes, 128 pages,
soft cover
ISBN: 0-88740-913-X $19.95